Milestones & Memories
A STROLL THROUGH TIME IN
West Haddon

an illustrated history by
WEST HADDON LOCAL HISTORY GROUP

First published 2000 by
West Haddon Local History Group
For information about the Group, please
contact the Hon. Secretary,
Sherry Calvert at
Ashleigh House, Crown Lane,
West Haddon,
Northants NN6 7AL

A CIP record is available from the British Library

Designed by: James Atkins Design, West Haddon
Edited by: Michael Clarke
Typeset in Sabon
Printed in the UK by: Caerprint, Cirencester
Printed on: Fedrigoni Sirio Smooth (text), Splendorgel (cover)
ISBN: 0-9538941-0-X

Contents

1 West Haddon in the early part
   of the last century   7

2 A West Haddon family:
   the Townleys   17

3 Church and chapel:
   religion in the village   25

4 Sipping and supping: the pubs, hostelries
   and hotels of West Haddon   31

5 Roots of the future:
   the Garrett family tree   37

6 The changing face of farming   43

7 A West Haddon family:
   the Heygates   51

8 Charity begins at home   55

9 Willingly to school   59

10 A changing century   73

Dedicated to the memory of John Raybould, 1941 – 2000. John and his wife Wendy were instrumental in setting up West Haddon Local History Group and started the collection of photographs which has made this book possible.

Acknowledgments

This book is intended as a record of some of the items researched by members of the West Haddon Local History Group. It is hoped that it will jog the memories of villagers and their friends and relatives who have moved away. The group is always eager for more information and photographs and is indebted to a great number of people who have allowed their photographs to be copied.

The group has always taken the view that material collected belongs to the village and has published several photocopied leaflets which served the purpose at the time but now look a little dated. Even history groups have to move with the times! A more professional approach was needed and the group was very fortunate to secure the services of James Atkins, a local designer who recently moved to the village. We hope you like the result.

Money was needed to put the book together at this professional level. Several avenues were tried but it was the National Lottery 'Awards for All' scheme which came up with the grant which has enabled the project to go ahead. It would also not have been possible without the services of Michael Clarke, another 'newcomer' who has patiently chivvied everyone along, edited the text and put together the application for the grant.

There are may people and groups whose help we would like to acknowledge, particularly Mrs Wendy Raybould, Mrs J M Lord, Mr K Croxford, Miss B Heygate, Mrs M Litchfield, Mrs E Litchfield, Mr K Sharpe, Mrs Windsor and West Haddon Primary School and the creators of the school website.

There has been a great deal of hype about the Millennium, but it has given the group the incentive to gather together this information and to get it published in a durable form. We hope that village projects will benefit from the sales of this book.

Locations of places mentioned in this book:

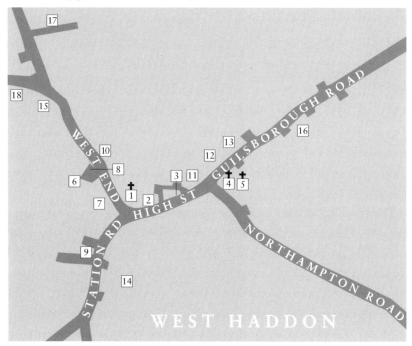

1	All Saints Church	10	Townley's Property
2	The Crown	11	The Pytchley Hotel
3	Manchester House	12	The Bell
4	Baptist Church	13	The Compass
5	Wesleyan Chapel (site of)	14	West Haddon Hall
6	West Haddon School	15	The Dun Cow
7	The Sheaf	16	The Grazier's Arms
8	The Red Lion (site of)	17	Bungalow Farm
9	The Spread Eagle	18	The Almshouses

1

West Haddon in the early part of the last century

Sherry Calvert

You've seen it all a hundred times, on the television or at the cinema – the first half of the 20th Century. It covers the Edwardian era, and Britain between the wars, but what was it like to live in West Haddon at that time? As you read this, you will almost certainly live in a house with all modern conveniences – running hot and cold water, and electricity. Possibly you have mains gas, which was not brought in to the village until 1992. Most houses have a telephone, television, washing machine, fridge, freezer, an oven or stove for cooking, probably a microwave oven, and central heating. Doesn't it create inconvenience when any one of them breaks down?

Older villagers can recall times when these were not the 'norm'. In 1851 the population of the village was 989. This had fallen to 753 in 1901 and continued to decline in the first half of the 20th Century as people left agricultural and horticultural work for employment in factories and offices in Rugby and Northampton.

In some ways, though, life in the village was richer. The village was much more self sufficient. Today, we count ourselves lucky that there are still shops which we need on an everyday basis – a Post Office with general goods, and a store with its own bakery and, perhaps most important, a National Lottery outlet. There are three pubs – The Pytchley Hotel, The

Sheaf and The Crown. The village specialises in antiques with three shops selling between them a wide range. On the edge of the village is a plant nursery and close by a lawn mower shop. Since the start of the 1990s, the village has 'lost' a clothes shop, an estate agent and a flower shop. Archive photographs tell how many more changes there have been in the last hundred years.

In the early part of the last century, it was very important to be near a bakehouse and there were several. One was Bush's *(fig.1)* in the High Street. Freddie Adams used to deliver bread from this shop using a pony and trap. There was another one in Station Road until the Second World War. The bakers had to get up early to start baking, around four o'clock in the morning. The last bakers were the Tyrells, who took over from Coopers and before that 'Fiddler' Cross. They used to deliver round the village, and also offered a roasting service. Between the wars, it would have cost you 2d (about 1p) on Sundays and 1d (^{1}/2p) during the week if you didn't have your own oven. You took your joint of meat on a meat stand, with potatoes underneath, round there for them to cook, especially on a Sunday whilst you were in church, and collected it later. Imagine doing that with a pizza!

The general store in the High Street *(fig.2)* was run by Freddie Spring of the Co-op, who came over from Long Buckby, until it closed, became *Matilda's* and is now *'Barber's Antiques'*. Most groceries were sold loose. Sugar and dry fruit were weighed into blue sugar bags for each customer according to their needs (or purse). Biscuits came in big tins but were also sold by the imperial pound (lb) in paper bags. Butter and lard were weighed and wrapped in greaseproof paper. At Christmas, good customers were given a small present to encourage trade, rather like supermarket loyalty cards. Then as now, regular customers were always sought after.

The general store in West End, next to The Sheaf, belonged to Tommy Adams before the First World War. It has changed hands regularly throughout the century.

Meat was supplied by one of several butchers. There was a slaughter-house in Crown Lane, by which is meant the road near to the church – the

figure 1: Bush's Bakehouse c. 1930s (now Paul Hopwell Antiques)

figure 2: General Store – High Street c.1920s

figure 3: Gil & Cliff York with the wooden 'fish & chip hut' in the background, 1935 – no advertising signs necessary!

other end of Crown Lane was known as 'Checkers Lane'. West Haddon had been on the 'drove road' the Middle Ages and cattle were 'rested' here on their way south.

Reg Cross ran his butcher's shop in the High Street handily close to the slaughter house. Possibly he slaughtered for all the butchers in the village. His shop was on the northern side of High Street, across Crown Lane, from The Crown. Today it is a garden wall but close inspection will reveal the blocked up doorways of the cottages which used to stand there. When the shop was condemned, he moved to premises by The Pytchley Hotel and also expanded his range of goods. Conditions would have been very different then. No environmental health officer checking for 'mad cow disease'. Food was stored in the pantry or larder. To keep it cool, the bottom shelves were brick, built up from the floor, with wooden top shelves. The walls were whitewashed.

There was another butchers at the top of Crown Lane, and one in the Shambles in West End, at one point run by the Judkins, of pork pie fame *(see chapter 3)*. The Judkins were cousins to the Tyrells at the Station Road bakehouse. There's nothing like keeping business within the family!

This butcher's definitely did not have its own slaughterhouse, but of course, it was more convenient for this part of the village to obtain meat here instead of further round in the High Street. Without refrigerated storage, it was necessary to buy at frequent intervals, which is why West Haddon could support so many butchers, in addition to the greater importance of red meat in the diet in the first part of the 20th Century.

Many families kept their own pig, and Reg Cross, the butcher, was one of the men who would turn up and kill it when required. Oliver Taylor, who lived in West Haddon, but worked in Rugby, could also be called upon. If you fancied a change from roast pork, Freddie Adams would make up pork pies for you.

Although there was not a fish shop in the village, Joe 'Fishy' Moore from Long Buckby came over in his Renault van twice a week and you could also get vegetables from him. The popular fish and chip shop at the back of the Sheaf, which was opened about 1924, was a sort of fast food outlet which was easily accessible to the whole village – fish cost tuppence (about 1p today) and chips a penny (1/2p). It was built of wood *(fig. 3)* and was run by Bill Adams, then Mrs Muddiman, then Madeleine York.

Potatoes were peeled in a barrel with a sort of nutmeg grater inside. A handle was attached to the barrel, which was filled with water. By turning the handle the potatoes tumbled inside it. However, it was still necessary to remove the eyes by hand. The chips were fried in dripping, and in later years, oil. Fish was collected in wooden boxes from Northampton – you had to catch the 8.00am Midland Red bus from The Crown, and come back on the 9.20. If they ran out of fish they fried anything else that came to hand! Madeleine Litchfield's parents kept poultry, so chicken and eggs were handy variations, and sausages got the same treatment. Marrowfat peas were soaked overnight, then boiled in a Judge enamel pan on a double gas burner. The whole lot was wrapped up and eaten out of newspaper. It wasn't necessary to have a sign outside the wooden hut – everyone knew where to get fish and chips. If you want fish and chips today, you can have them on a Wednesday evening when the coach comes round. On other days you must drive into Long Buckby.

What about the sweetie shop? One of ours was in Station Road: Mr and Mrs Burns ran the business from their front room and retired upstairs to their living room in between customers. Mr Burns used to put chicken mesh wire over the counter to stop birds stealing the sweets and it took time to get down to answer the bell. Groceries were also sold here as was beer, which was quite common for sweet shops. Miss Jelley (appropriately) had a shop in West End, where you get such delights as 'everlasting sticks' (dream on!) and bulls eyes. Nancy Adams' grandmother used to make her own boiled sweets to sell – an entrepreneurial granny. There was also a sweet shop in West End near the butcher's.

Sweets tended to be a once a week treat rather than a case of hopping off the school bus and indulging on the way home! Ice cream, too, was a treat because you simply could not store it. Commerford's ice cream was produced at Northampton before and after (but not during) the Second World War, and Wall's ice cream was brought round on a tricycle on

Sunday afternoons. There was only a choice of strawberry, vanilla or almond – no Ben and Jerry's then! In fact, refrigeration was such a novelty in the first half of the 20th Century that one villager remembers feeling faint and being offered a cooled glass of water to revive her.

Milk was supplied by several farmers, who, of course, hand milked. Atterbury's had a milk round, which was taken over by Arthur Vines; so did Harry Farn at the saddlers in the High Street opposite the Church, next to where Spencer Court is today. He milked his own herd and delivered, but usually about midnight! He is remembered as having a beard, wearing a trilby and snacking all day on bread and butter pudding. He had a wife who played the piano and a daughter who spoke seven languages and married a Portuguese Count.

Milk was brought to the houses in large pails which were filled from the churns. It was then ladled into villagers' own jugs. As bottles came in to use (and were one of the first items to be recycled regularly) farms had their names printed on to them. Samples of Atterbury's bottles survive. As well as the Atterbury family, Harry Farn and Bill Clarke all brought their herds into West Haddon to be milked, and members of the Rugby Cycling Club said in 1946 that the village had the dirtiest roads they knew – this was traffic calming on a major scale!

The village has always been plentifully supplied with water even though it is situated on the side of a hill and there are no streams. Many houses in the High Street and West End still have their own well and cellars flood during rain storms. There were five public pumps around the village and several private ones. The public pump in Northampton Road remains but in a state of disrepair today. There was also one in Crown Lane by The Pytchley Hotel, one in Watford Road, and a spring on The Green. The District Council eventually took over the water supply which is fed by gravity to the village. However, when the 'new' council houses were built in Guilsborough Road, pressure was insufficient to supply them until a water tower was built.

Until mains sewage was provided in the 1950s, most cottages had a toilet just outside the kitchen door or at the bottom of the garden often referred

12

to as 'bogs'. A wooden seat was provided sometimes with two holes! Imagine sitting there side by side. These toilets had to be emptied once a year – some men undertook this task to earn beer money. Some houses had 'water closets', but water had to be fetched in buckets from the pump.

Hot water was obtained by lighting the boiler fires for the women to do the washing in a 'copper'. Rubbish was burned as fuel in the 'copper hole'. Miss Osborne, who lived in a cottage on The Green would take in washing for you. Hot water for the tin baths, filled and emptied by bucket, was also needed. Lighting by gas or electricity was not generally available until the 1920s.

Local road sweepers kept the roads as best they could. Bertie French swept the roads in the 20s and 30s, and Cecil Franks was the other sweeper. Carriers such as Highams at 'The Shambles' brought the mail to and from Rugby. The village 'looked' to Rugby – some addresses were given as 'West Haddon, near Rugby', as Northampton was considered too far and Daventry too difficult to get to. Having said that, Daventry was where you walked to get your 'dole' (unemployment benefit) until an office opened in Long Buckby. Another carrier was Mr Looker from Yelvertoft, with a horse drawn vehicle. He also had a solid tyred lorry with forms round the side. Local businessmen obviously saw traffic increasing as a garage was built in the 1920s on the site now occupied by Spencer Court in the High Street. It was originally owned by Harry Flack – the children used to shout "Flacky get your Ford out and take us for a ride!" such was the novelty. There weren't many cars in the 1920s!

Latterly, the garage was owned by Chapman and finally Heep, by which time it was known just as Heeps *(fig. 4)*. Mr Chapman built the workshop extension at the rear using an ex World War One army surplus roof. The canopy to the east of the garage was built by Condor and when erected, was the biggest in the country. It was also higher than the normal 12 –13 feet, with 18 feet (about 5.5 metres) of clearance so that combine harvesters could get in and out. There was some difficulty getting planning permission from the Council.

If you hadn't got a car, you had to get on your bike, and Mr Hutchins at

figure 4: Heeps Garage c. 1970s

Clover Cottage in the High Street rented them out, mended punctures and sold spares as well. The pony and trap were still widely in use, and one villager remembers her whole family of four travelling in a motorbike and sidecar in 1920. By then there were quite a few hardy folk who cycled daily to and from Rugby to work.

The boot and shoe industry flourished in the area and you could get your footwear repaired either by Mr Orland, who worked in a room above the grocery store in West End, or at Scotty Letts' round the back of the Red Lion which stood on the Green. At one time a Mr Huckle lived in Manchester House *(fig. 5)* and he too, would mend for you. Manchester House was generally associated with textiles – 'Manchester goods', i.e. cotton. It was kept by Frank Underwood before World War I, followed by Parkers. Opinion divides as the whether he sold or repaired shoes. Mrs Cecily Ainge was acknowledged as a good needlewoman, and there was a drapery shop in West End – which also used to sell toys upstairs at Christmas. Villagers remember it heated by oil stoves which made patterns on the ceiling.

Life for tradesmen was, in some ways, a little more leisurely in those days. A local story tells of Bill Ward, a hairdresser in Long Buckby, who once left a customer in a chair with his hair half cut, while he delivered something to West Haddon by bus!

Many villagers grew their own food in their gardens and allotments but the village has a history of horticulture which was more specialised and served a wider market. Fred Ainge lived in Vine Cottage, in Guilsborough Road, and ran his own nursery in Northampton Road, where the council houses now stand. A nursery belonging to Mr Harris which employed a number of villagers was further up Northampton Road. A third, in West End was run by Frank and Beryl Lee (Auntie Beryl).

As the number of cars has increased, West Haddon has changed in character. Many people now commute short and long distances. News heard over the radio by villagers is no longer shown on a note in the window of the baker's as it once was – a different sort of Neighbourhood Watch! The fact that we still have the shops that we do is probably attributable to the A428 running through the village. It remains to be seen whether a bypass is built and, if it is, what effect this will have on the village and the services it provides for itself and visitors.

2 A West Haddon family – the Townleys

Liz Parker

In the 19th Century two families named Townley came to West Haddon to live and work. The only connection between them was a dressmaker from Southam, Warwickshire called Leah Louisa Warwick…

A non-conformist tailor – John Townley

John Townley, born in 1805 in Maidwell, followed in his father's footsteps and became a tailor. This was the year of Nelson's victory at the Battle of Trafalgar and George III had been on the throne for forty five years. We are not sure when John Townley came to West Haddon, but he was living here by the early 1820s. In 1828 he bought some property in the High Street[1], a draper's shop with parlour (now known as Manchester House) and four cottages with gardens, mostly rented out to tenants. He chose to live, with his wife Maria, in Manchester House. John probably made only men's clothing, for example coats, waistcoats and breeches, from flannel or worsted. Shirts were usually made at home from linen, rather than by the village tailor. In the mid 19th Century there were three tailors in the village.

John and Maria had three children, Martha Abbott (born 1830), James (1832) and John Abbott (1835). All the children were baptised in the Wesleyan faith. The Wesleyan Chapel (*fig. 6*), in Guilsborough Road, had a Sunday School as did all Wesleyan chapels because non-conformist children did not attend Church of England schools until education was

[1] Deed dated 30th April 1829

made compulsory in the 1860s. This resulted in non-conformist churches setting up Sunday Schools in order to teach their children to read and write. John's business continued to expand and by 1844 he had borrowed a further £550[2] (£22,000 in today's value). This may have been the time when he had the stone lettering carved on the front of his house *(fig. 5&7)*. We do not know who produced the stonework, but John Johnson, builder and mason, had bought the property opposite (now known as Lime House) in 1822, so it is possible that the carving is his work.

John took on apprentices: John Barrett, aged 15, was employed in 1841, and William Egglestone in 1871.

In 1854, James, the elder son, died aged twenty two years. Martha married William Dunmore in late 1859 and moved to Maidwell, the village where her father was born. She also followed in her father's footsteps being described in the 1881 census as a tailoress. By that time she was a widow living in Deptford, Kent, with her five children, and her eldest daughter was also a dressmaker.

We think that Maria Townley died in the late 1860s, possibly around the time that Leah Louisa Warwick came to West Haddon from Southam to work as a draper's assistant. We don't know why she came to West Haddon, but she may have had relatives in the village. In the 1871 census she is listed as John's niece and, with her sister Emma (also a draper's assistant), as living in John Townley's household. Although Leah Louisa is always described as John's niece, there is an endorsement in John's will to the effect that she is 'erronousely described as the niece of the testator'. She must, however, have become a close companion of John, as his will, dated December 28th, 1876, bequeaths his entire estate (except for two small legacies to his surviving children) to Leah Louisa. John died in 1878 and his household effects were worth less than £100. Along with the tailoring business, Leah Louisa also inherited his debts, which were £350 (plus five percent interest per annum), originally lent by Charles Nicholas W Parsons. Leah Louisa continued the business, living in Manchester House

[2] Mortgages dated September 8th 1835, May 19th 1836 & January 30th 1839

figure 5: Manchester House (furthest right with awnings) c. 1920s

figure 6: The Wesleyan Chapel (top left) with the Baptist Church (bottom right)

figure 7: Manchester House 2000. It is likely that the painted sign on the house shown in fig. 5 says 'Boothby'. It was a surprise when recent renovations exposed the the legend 'Townley Tailor & Draper'

with her daughter Louisa Osborne (she named her daughter after herself and her mother's maiden name), her brother Eli (described in 1881 as an Army Pensioner), and her niece, Emma Maria Jordan (the daughter of her sister, Mary Ann). In 1882 she had repaid £50 of the debt[3], just before she married George Lewis Townley (Chappie) and went to live in West End. She probably continued to run the drapery business at the Manchester House shop. In 1890 she conveyed the property[4] to the executors of Charles Parsons (who had died in 1885) – perhaps because she was unable to repay the debt in full.

When Leah Louisa died in 1897, apart from two legacies to her daughter (£500 on reaching 21 years old plus all monies in her bank account) and to her niece Emma Maria Jordan (£100), she left her entire estate (the drapery business is not mentioned separately in the will) to her husband George. It's likely that Emma Maria continued to work in the draper's shop and she later became George Lewis Townley's second wife. Until recently, older villagers could remember Emma Townley selling haberdashery from Manchester House at the turn of the last century.

In 1901 George repaid the Parsons debt and became the owner of the property[5], later selling it to George Frederick Letts. Sometime after that it becomes Archie Underwood's cobbler shop, and it is now a private house.

George Lewis Townley – An entrepreneurial blacksmith

George Lewis Townley – known affectionately as 'Chappie', (fig.8) one-time blacksmith, and later, hydraulic engineer and property developer, was born in West Haddon, in 1855. Queen Victoria had been on the throne for eighteen years and it was four years before Darwin published 'On the Origin of Species'. Chappie's parents were Daniel, a blacksmith (probably in West End, near The Green), from Long Buckby, and Anne, an antique dealer. He was the third of six sons, five of whom were brought up to be blacksmiths. The second son, Daniel, emigrated to Australia and in 1886 he made a

---

[3] Deed dated 9th October 1897
[4] Conveyance dated 21st October 1890
[5] Conveyance dated 18th September 1901

swing plough and a two horse plough which won first and second prizes for a farmer in an agricultural show in New South Wales[6]. When Chappie was sixteen years old, he made a working model of an engine from scraps in the family's blacksmith shop[7]. Two years later he was helping to run his father's business. However, by the 1870s, the trade of blacksmithing was in decline. The Grand Union canal and the railway had been open many years and were taking an increasing share of the transport of goods around the country and factories in Sheffield were churning out mass produced good quality steel tools, much cheaper than the local village blacksmith. Most villages had at least two or three smithies – at this time in West Haddon the other was Henry Booker in Guilsborough Road. Perhaps as a result of the declining trade, Chappie decided to diversify into the manufacture and installation of hydraulic rams and he set up the Ram Water Works in the early 1870s. A ram is a simple device (not requiring an electricity supply) for pumping water up to a tank *(fig.9)*. Water from the top tank is then fed by gravity to houses. He installed the first ram at Winwick Warren in about 1875. He also supplied hydraulic rams to local gentry, notably Earl Spencer at Althorp Park and the Hon. E A Fitzroy MP, Speaker of the House of Commons, at Foxhill. West Haddon Hall and several farmers also bought them. Although the ram was originally invented and patented in 1774, Chappie was obviously an inventive man himself, as in 1897 he patented an improvement for producing the steady flow of water[8]. The business, which had started as a simple smithy, was now a successful hydraulic engineering company employing about fifty men.

By the turn of the century he was also making and selling sawhorses. An advert describes them as 'Pitch Pine with Ash saw frame, Varnished £1-16s-6d' (£88 in today's value).

In 1883, when he was twenty eight years old, Chappie married Leah Louisa Warwick. Although Leah Louisa was born in Southam she had

[6] *Northampton Herald 12th June 1886*
[7] *Obituary of George Lewis Townley in local paper*
[8] *Patent Office No. 10414*

figure 8: George Townley,
c.1900

figure 9: George Townley's hydraulic ram,
c.1900

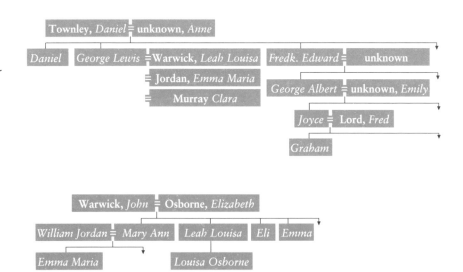

figure 10: The Townley and Warwick family trees

22

already been living here in John Townley's household, for about fifteen years, was thirty nine years old and had one daughter, Louisa Osborne Warwick, aged six.

It is likely that at this time Chappie purchased the property in West End for his family and business. The property, built in the early 1800s and called 'The Park' consisted of a house (at the front), which he renovated for the family home, and a single storey workshop. Later Chappie converted the workshop and added a second storey to provide a new residence, which became known as 'The Old House'. He didn't actually do the work himself, as he had lost an arm in an accident at a sawmill, which was probably in the wheelwright's shop on his own premises. He also renovated other houses in the village and was fond of installing gable windows.

As well as engineering work, Chappie and his father also did some part time work as census enumerators, Daniel covering the whole village in 1881. By 1891, Daniel was sixty six years old and could only manage the south side, while his son walked around the north.

When Leah Louisa died aged fifty three, apart from the small bequests to her daughter and niece, she left all her possessions and estate (about £900) to Chappie. This mainly consisted of the property Manchester House, which she had inherited from John Townley, the tailor.

A few years later Chappie married again, to Emma Maria Jordan. She was the daughter of Leah Louisa's sister, Mary Ann, and had been born in Southam in 1863. When Emma died in 1920 at Northampton General Hospital, Chappie bought a small piece of land[9] next to the Baptist Chapel which he donated in memory of Emma. The land is on the west side and is now planted as a garden.

Chappie is remembered by many older villagers as being a generous, if eccentric man. For one royal celebration (probably the coronation of King George V in 1911), he bought mugs and gave one to each schoolchild. One of the contributors to this book remembers when, sometime in the 1920s, he bought a crate of oranges, and gave one to each child as they came out

[9] *Conveyance dated 1st October 1920 (Baptist Union Trustees)*

of school.

In the late 1920s, he married for the third and last time, to Clara Murray, a widow of Northampton. She already had two daughters, Clarissa and 'Tot'. He built a house in Crick Road, called Oak Tree Cottage, and went to live there until he died, aged 81, in 1936. The house was known locally as 'Jail House', because Chappie had bought prison doors from Northampton Jail when it was demolished and used them to fence the property.

In his will[10], he left Clara Oak Tree Cottage, plus four acres, his household goods and his motor car. He also left a legacy of £1000 to St. Cross Hospital in Rugby for a named bed. His nephew, George Albert, inherited Ivy Cottage, the house behind it known as 'Ye Olde Cottage' and another four cottages in the High Street. His friend and employee, Frederick 'Joe' Adams, a carpenter, received £500.

The funeral was arranged by his employees and held at the village Church. There were many beautiful wreaths sent by his family and friends. George and his first two wives, Leah Louisa and Emma Maria, are buried in the churchyard.

Although Chappie married three times he had no children of his own. After he died the business was carried on first by his nephew, George Albert, then George Albert's son-in-law, Fred Lord and finally, Fred's son, Graham. In 1998 Chappie's great niece Joyce Lord and her son Graham retired and left the village.

In the year 2000 there are no longer any Townleys living in West Haddon.

[10] *Will dated 22nd March 1935, probate 11th May 1936*

3 Church and Chapel: religion in the village

Hilda Stanley

In common with many villages, West Haddon has a thriving church and chapel, which have formed the hub of the village's social life as well as being places of worship. The parish church of All Saints *(fig.11)* still stands high above the village centre and remains a busy, active church and community focus. The Baptist chapel, further up on Guilsborough Road, is also in regular use. There was also once a Wesleyan place of worship, now gone and long gone *(fig.6)*.

The parish church is built of stone and is a combination of Norman, Decorated and Perpendicular styles, with a chancel, clerestoried nave, south porch and embattled tower. There was once a spire here but it fell into decay and was taken down in 1648. The tower contains a clock and five bells, the oldest of which is dated 1611.

The main part of the church dates from the 14th Century, and the heavy door, with its studs and ironwork and massive lock and key was there a hundred years before the Battle of Agincourt. One of the church's treasures, a rare Norman font – cubical with a band of carving around the upper part and hollowed from a block of stone *(fig. 12)*, is a lucky survivor as fonts became unpopular during the Reformation of the Church in England, in the 16th Century, and many were smashed. Perhaps this one survived as it was originally built into the west wall, beneath the gallery.

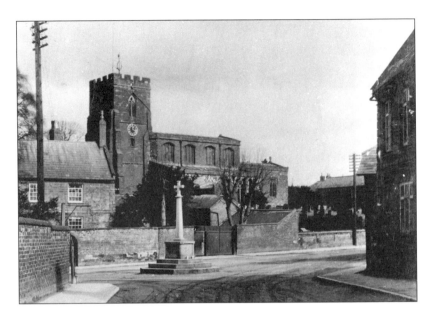

figure 11: All Saints church with the war memorial in its original location. pre-1960s

Many English churches were extensively restored during the Victorian 'religious revival'. While some of the changes were undoubtedly beneficial, such as better heating systems and gas or electric lighting, others damaged or destroyed relics of the past with ill-considered renovation. An example is the open timber roof of the nave, from the 15th Century, which has been 'restored' and lost much of its original decoration. A 'three decker' pulpit was taken down in 1889 when the present pulpit was installed – 'three deckers' are now extremely rare: in fact, one of the few remaining examples can be seen in nearby Ashby St. Legers. The removal of the pulpit was part of the first of two 'restorations' of the church: the first, from 1887–94, cost £2,000 while the second, in 1908, was more modest in scope and cost £500. The oak reredos and roodscreen were designed by Mr Bligh Bond and erected in 1909 and 1910 respectively.

A number of notable local families are commemorated in the church. As well as the Heygate family vault (*chapter 7*), there is a tablet to John

Heygate, who built and endowed the village school. Other families recalled include the Slyes, who have two memorial windows to their name, and Henry Atterbury Esq., to whom the East Window, installed at a cost of £102, is dedicated.

Life as a parish priest was often hard. The blocked up window above the tower's arch is at the level of a chamber now occupied by the church clock. Before the Reformation, parish priests were expected to be celibate, and West Haddon's would have lived in this chamber – he would have been able to conduct his night offices without descending into the church. The earliest recorded incumbent was Walter Capellan, in 1209. Later clergy would have the benefit of a 'living' – a discharged vicarage with one acre of glebeland. Near the south wall in the churchyard can be seen the tomb of Griggory Palmer, who was born in the village in 1609 and was its distinguished vicar from 1641 to 1693. The original doggrel inscription reads:

> *Here lyeth honest Griggory,*
> *Which was a true friend to the Ministry;*
> *And the soul's true friend for eternity,*
> *And one of the best of fathers to his ability;*
> *He studied the true form of Christianity,*
> *The which he hoped would abound to posterity.*

While the Parish Church is celebrated for its fine features, and distinguished incumbents, life at the Baptist chapel seems to have been more notable for its social scene. The Women's Bright Hour, the Men's Bible Study Class and the Christian Endeavour were all extremely popular. Rev. Hearn *(fig.13)* was minister there in the early part of the 20th Century, and he and his wife, who were childless, seem to have enjoyed playing a major role in organising parties, 'socials' and gatherings, where games such as 'Postman's Knock' and 'spinning the plate' were played.

A social committee, consisting of fourteen ladies, raised money in many ways: as well as the traditional jumble sales, concerts and sales of work, they would bake pork pies which sold for a shilling (5p) each. The pork

figure 12: Norman font,
All Saints church

figure 13: Rev. Hearn & his wife. Minister
of West Haddon Baptist Church. 1928

was bought from Mr Judkin, the butcher, and the ladies, wearing spotless white aprons, would assemble the pies complete with jelly and crust. They were then baked and all were spoken for before they were out of the ovens. At the annual general meeting, the committee had a meal beforehand, which consisted of as much pork pie and bread and butter as you could eat, for which the charge was one shilling and sixpence (about 8p) per head.

The social committee and the Sunday School ran a concert party which was very popular and much in demand in other villages in the area. Travelling by bike or on foot – for there were no buses in those days – they performed at Guilsborough, Cold Ashby, Welford and Rugby, where they entertained the inmates of the workhouse, who sat with the men on one side of the hall and the women on the other. On one occasion, a measles epidemic threatened the concert party's performance, until one young lady learned three parts at great speed! At Christmas, the concert party went carol singing in the village, usually ending up at the Manse around midnight, where Mrs Hearn ensured a plentiful supply of much needed refreshment. The concert party is still fondly remembered by older village residents today.

The Hearns were followed by other ministers who continued the tradition of active social programmes to complement the chapel's religious work. This continued unabated until 1939, but since the war, cinema, television and better transportation contributed to a decline in the social life of the chapel. However, the efforts of its members and adherents ensure that life still goes on.

One of the chapel's members, in the years before the war, Mr Charles Orland, was baptised in the traditional method – by total immersion – at the age of sixteen. He recalls that it was quite an event: the baptistry had to be filled and, as there was no running water, chapel members had to go to the village pump with buckets. A copperful of hot water would be put into the tub immediately prior to the baptism 'to take the chill off', as the old folk said.

4

Sipping and supping: the pubs, hostelries and hotels of West Haddon

Synopsis of original publication by
West Haddon Local History Group

Visitors to West Haddon may be surprised to find three thriving, but quite different pubs/hotels in a relatively small village; however in the past there have been many alehouses and pubs important in the life of the village.

Ale has always been an important beverage in England. Brewing was one of the kitchen arts, like baking. Medieval ale didn't keep well, so neighbours might take it in turns to produce a batch to avoid waste. A widow would make supplies to sell in order to support herself and family.

Village ale-houses began selling beer for consumption at home or out in the fields. It was not until time of Queen Elizabeth I that villagers adopted the habits of townspeople and gathered in the alehouse to drink and socialise with others. Even so, alehouses were still part-time affairs and their keepers had other occupations for bringing in income. In the 18th Century the alehouses widened their scope and began to offer cheap imported drinks, notably gin. Legislation was introduced to try and stamp out gin drinking, particularly the Beerhouse Act of 1830, which made it much easier for householders to obtain licences for beer only and so small beerhouses began to proliferate in villages like West Haddon.

The first brewers and alehouse keepers shown in records of West Haddon were Robert Newman and John Lynnell who both paid fines for transgressing local bylaws (Assize of Ale) in October 1581. These were the first West Haddon brewers known by name but there must have been people producing alcoholic beverages here for centuries before this.

By 1630, the alehouse was becoming a regular feature of West Haddon life and at this time alehouse licences were granted to three people: Henry Newman, Robert's son; Thomas Jenoway, and Isobel Murcote, one of whom may have operated on the market. The Newman family continued its connection with alehouses and there is a likely link through to the sale to John Gulliver of The Cock, and which we know now as The Sheaf.

The first identifiable alehouses in records occur around 1715 to 1740 with The Cock, and The Crown, which was owned by John West. However, alehouse keeping was perhaps still not seen as a steady way of earning a living and John West, for instance, combined it with tailoring. A third alehouse was also known at this time, The Red Lion, *(fig.14)* which was run by the Burbidge family.

The Red Lion became the principal inn of the village, hosting a variety of official gatherings, most notably the Turnpike Trustees who were concerned with improving the awful state of the main road between Rugby and Northampton. As the road improved it was used more and West Haddon saw an increasing amount of traffic rattling through the village and more people stopping off for refreshments at The Red Lion.

There was much rivalry between The Crown *(fig.15)*, John West and family, and The Red Lion, Mary Burbidge and family, through the remainder of the 18th Century, with both competing for business in the village. This went on until the bankruptcy of Mary Burbidge. John West bought The Red Lion and put it out of business in 1800.

New establishments came and went. The end of The Red Lion left something of a vacuum in the village but at about this time Richard Turner, a tailor, took out his first licence for The Spread Eagle in Station Road, and we begin to hear about The Dun Cow, in West End.

Some of these were short lived: The Dun Cow disappeared on the death of its owner, Richard Baucutt. The Spread Eagle did continue into the 1800s, but The Bell, set up after the 1830 Beerhouse Act, failed to survive the growth of the Temperance movement, positioned as it was between the

Wesleyan and Baptist Chapels.

For the first half of the 19th Century, both The Sheaf and The Crown thrived, and in 1840, The Sheaf was bought by a Northampton brewer. Around this time we also hear of The Compass. West Haddon, in 1841, had a population of over a thousand, but accommodation for travellers was short and John West, a cousin of The Crown's John West, began to take in lodgers. His business did well and he took off the old thatched roof and raised the house walls to a full three storeys, and inserted the date stone to commemorate the improvement in 1862. You can see it on the wall of the old Compass in Guilsborough Road.

Meanwhile graziers were raising more livestock for the London market and Welsh drovers were herding their cattle through the village creating the need for somewhere to sleep overnight. A farmhouse on the edge of the village became The Grazier's Arms. *(fig.16)*

One by one the pubs ceased to be run by individual owners and were sold off to the growing commercial breweries of Northampton. The Sheaf

figure 14: 'The Red Lion' at the corner of
The Green and West End

figure 15: 'The Crown' c.1920s

figure 16: 'The Grazier's Arms' which burned down in the 1970s

went to Thomas Haggar of the Northampton Brewery in 1838; The Crown to Phipps in 1879 and The Grazier's Arms to the Northampton Brewery in 1879 and then to Phipps in 1959. The Spread Eagle meanwhile, went to the Long Buckby Brewery.

With agricultural depression at the end of the Century the population of the village fell, but on the whole the pubs thrived. The Crown was used for a variety of social gatherings, including square dances organised by Nurse Muncaster to raise funds for the village hall. When old Mrs Atterbury of Manor Farm died, a funeral dinner was laid on at The Sheaf for the farm workers. When the Second World War came, The Compass was used as a meeting place for the Home Guard. After the war Westfield House became the Westfield Hotel, and is now The Pytchley Hotel.

The Pytchley, Sheaf and Crown have survived, but the beerhouses are gone: The Spread Eagle closed after the war and The Compass only survived until the 1960s. The Grazier's, sadly, was destroyed by fire during a major refurbishment in the 1970s. The Dun Cow, The Red Lion and The Bell are long gone, probably with others whose names are now forgotten.

Now the village population is growing again, pubs and hotels continue to provide a place to gather and socialise, and in these days a place to eat out with family and friends. With leisure time increasing they will continue to play a strong role in village life.

5

Roots of the future:
the Garrett family tree

A J Garrett

Many of my father's forebears lived in West Haddon during the 19th Century, although he himself was born and bred in East Haddon. He married a Long Buckby girl and they eventually settled in that village. West Haddon, which was long associated with my ancestors, seemed a rather mysterious place to me as a child and, though often spoken of, was never visited, for none of my living relatives resided there. At that time West Haddon and Long Buckby were largely self-sufficient villages, with shops, schools and services to meet most residents' requirements.

One United Counties bus route to Northampton began at West Haddon, picked up passengers at Long Buckby and proceeded, via East Haddon, to 'town'. The return journey gave a Long Buckby traveller great views of the rolling Northamptonshire countryside, but he always alighted before West Haddon was reached. Only on rare occasions, when the Midland Red 'X96' was used to travel from the 'Why Not' Inn, near Buckby Folly, to Rugby and beyond, was West Haddon glimpsed.

I was born in Boat Yard, East Street, Long Buckby, just before the Second World War, and I realise now that I was privileged to be a part of a rural Northamptonshire way of life that had existed for generations but had disappeared forever by the 1950s. My memories of family gatherings centre on visits to Church Brampton, Chapel Brampton and East Haddon,

figure 17:
*Wedding of Alfred John (Jack) Garrett
and Kate Muddiman*

where most of my father's family lived.

My interest in local history probably stems from living in an area steeped in 'the past', and where still, little effort is required to imagine the ancient Britons at Borough Hill, the Romans on Watling Street, or the great Civil War battle at Naseby. My first attempt to construct a family tree, based on my own knowledge of my relatives, extended only to my grandparents. I had no idea of my great grandfather's first name, or how many siblings he

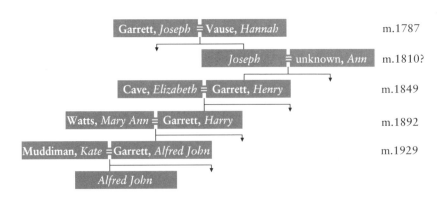

figure 18: The Garrett family tree

had, so I decided to concentrate my initial search on my grandfather, Harry Garrett, who died, aged 80, in 1950.

I began at the Office for National Statistics (now the Family Records Centre) where, unfortunately, only indexes, not the full certificates registering births, marriages and deaths, are held. Garrett is not an uncommon surname and Harry not an unusual forename, and, from what was available, I was unable to identify a birth record of a Harry Garrett in the Daventry registration district, which included West Haddon, where I assumed my grandfather was born. Here was my first lesson in genealogy – check everything and never assume!

The mystery of my grandfather's birth was solved when I turned to the census returns. The 1871 return shows no Harry Garrett in West Haddon, but ten years later, in the 1881 census, Harry Garrett, a scholar aged ten, appears as the son of Henry and Elizabeth Garrett, and is listed as born in Arnesby, Leicestershire. The 1871 census for Arnesby confirms that the Garretts and ten month old Harry were indeed resident in Main Street at that time. Armed with this information, I was able to request a copy of my grandfather's birth certificate, which gave a wealth of further information – including maiden name of the mother, and occupation of the father.

Encouraged by this success, I made several visits to the Family Records Centre and, after much laborious scanning of microfilms and heaving index volumes, I slowly began to gather the 'trunk' of the 'tree'. Other sources included the Northamptonshire Record Office, Northampton Library and the Church of Jesus Christ of the Latterday Saints in Harlestone Road, Northampton. All had a wealth of material – for example, I found in the library a copy of the West Haddon Parish Church magazine from 1898, which notes .the burial of my great grandfather, Henry Garrett, and that he died in Slye's Cottage after a short illness; while the West Haddon Parish Church registers, held at the Record Office, helped me extend my list of close family relatives.

I spent a pleasant hour one summer afternoon walking around the beautifully kept village churchyard, and found four headstones commemorating Garretts, but none with any direct connections to my own known ancestors. Most intriguing was one dedicated to 'Thomas Garrett, the Old Barber, died 1877, aged 77'.

Coming into contact with the West Haddon Local History Group was a crucial step forward: I discovered an organisation with an amazing collection of pictorial and documentary evidence about village life in the last two hundred years. Here was an opportunity to add local historical facts to family details. One of the group members, Mrs Wendy Raybould, kindly extracted from her own records a mass of references to Garretts, covering the 17th and 18th Centuries, including an extensive branch of the Garrett family tree!

So who were the Garretts of West Haddon? Where did they come from, were they all related, and where are their descendants? My father's family were certainly established in the village at the end of the 18th Century and remained at least until my great grandfather died in 1898. I have tentatively plotted my direct descent through five generations from Joseph and Hannah, who were married in 1787. The task was complicated, in that the Garretts obviously flourished during the 19th Century and they were unimaginative in the choice of forenames, with various Josephs, Henrys and Elizabeths with irritatingly close birthdates. In the middle of the 19th Century there were forty or so Garretts in residence in the village; by 1891, the census shows this had dropped to eleven. There are none on the current electoral register. Not all Garretts listed (and there are variations on spelling – Garret and Garratt also occurring) appear in the tree I have drawn so far *(fig.18)*.

Like most of their fellow villagers, my ancestors were in rural employment common to the region – 'Ag. Lab.' in the shorthand of the census officer – but only in the case of my great grandfather can I suggest an employer. In 1891, Henry lived with his wife Elizabeth and son Harry in Slye's Cottage, and presumably worked on William Walter Slye's farm. Harry may also have been employed by Slye, but must have departed, perhaps after his marriage to Mary Ann Watts in 1892, to set up home in East Haddon. Certainly, Grandfather Harry referred to himself as a shepherd, but I can recall him only as a kindly old man living quietly in retirement with his wife in East Haddon. He is pictured, *(fig. 17)* at the wedding of his son, my father in 1929.

Although the Garrett name has disappeared from West Haddon, the family connection continues in at least one household – my cousin, Christine Perryman, having moved to the village after her marriage, can look out over the fields that several generations of our family tended.

6

The changing face of farming

Ken & Jean Bailey and Madeleine Litchfield
talking to Annie Ballantyne

If you had lived in West Haddon during the early 20th Century, the surrounding fields, mostly in the ownership of small farmers, would have been mainly put to pasture, peacefully grazed by cattle and sheep. Much of the land in this area gives good grazing. Store cattle were regularly brought up from Wales to fatten locally on Summer grazing. The field names around the village illustrate our history: 'Buttit Meadow', 'Dairy Field', 'Hovel Meadow'...

Pre-war drovers, helped by two dogs, would walk fifty cattle through the village to markets in Northampton and Rugby. Advance warning to householders en route to close their front doors was absolutely necessary to avoid unwelcome animal visitors!

Perhaps we should also reflect on earlier changes in farming practices. In 1765 the old medieval open fields were enclosed, giving us the landscape we know today. Many of the small independent cottage craftsmen were no longer able to supplement their incomes with the produce from common grazing, or supply themselves with winter fuel from West Haddon Heath. Many of those with just an acre of two of their own found it made more economic sense to rent it out to a larger farmer for a cash rent, or to sell it outright and move elsewhere, where the market for goods was larger. So, after enclosure, farms became bigger.

There were many advantages to the ridge and furrow system in the age before mechanical equipment. It provided natural drainage, with land drains necessary only at the bottom of the field. The ridges also provided dry resting and feeding for wintering sheep and cattle, and faster drying of hay during haymaking. And for early recognition of greater productivity, a ridge and furrow system provided an extra bit of land each acre over flat land! Each year's ploughing set the ridge with a comfortable distance for the horse to turn, and the rhythmic swing of the hand scythe was easier to regulate up the ridge than working on the flat. Ridge and furrow fields are still grazed today around the southern and western boundaries to the village.

West Haddon's growth in the 16th and 17th centuries took advantage of the improved roads and an abundant supply of local wool. Conditions were ideal for a predominantly agricultural community to be transformed into a thriving little wool town. It was served by the mercers and chandlers who became full-time shopkeepers, and the inns and alehouses offering refreshment to travellers along the route of the turnpike. By the 19th Century the village had left its wool boom behind. The coming of the canal and the railway brought new prosperity to neighbouring Long Buckby, and West Haddon would not again be dominated by one industry or trade.

The 1881 Census of West Haddon parish illustrates the great variance in the occupations of rural dwellers then and now. There was then a population of 895, of which 57% was born in the village. Farmers numbered sixteen, with 113 agricultural labourers, ten shepherds and two graziers, plus the related occupations of miller, threshing machine owner, four carrier/waggoners and four wheelwrights. Four cattle dealers lived in the village, five blacksmiths and sixteen boot and shoe makers.

At the start of the 20th Century the usual farm wage was thirteen shillings per week; by 1939 it had risen to thirty shillings. After the First World War the nature of the village gradually changed, most noticeably during the 1930s when many working people left agriculture to take up new jobs in large manufacturing firms in Northampton, Rugby and Coventry, served by a then excellent network of bus services.

For those remaining in farming, local farmers bred and raised cattle and sheep and kept at least a few cows for milking. Farmers sold the milk either locally or sent it off in churns daily to the independent dairies in Northampton. Madeleine Litchfield, whose husband Bob, and his father Joe before him *(fig. 21)*, farmed at Grange Farm along the Yelvertoft Road, remembers the churns being taken over the fields to the Crick road by pony and float before the farm road was constructed. Timed to coincide with the arrival of the lorry, an impatient pony was remembered often to have walked off with the float of empty churns if conversation lasted too long.

In a free market, dairies faced with a summer surplus could refuse supplies from farmers. The coming of the Milk Marketing Board (MMB) in the mid 30s would change that. All milk not sold locally would have a guaranteed market, bought by the MMB and sold onto dairies, the surplus taken up for butter and cheese making. Farmers countrywide received a standard price irrespective of the price paid by the MMB to the dairies.

For economy, farmers were helped to replace churns with tanker collection about 20 years ago, and the familiar sight of churns stacked by the roadside would become another memory.

The MMB existed until 1994 when the European Community deemed it to be a monopoly and encouraged the government to disband it. Farmers were then free to sell to either what remained of the MMB or to independent dairies. Small farmers were to be penalised, by higher collection charges for smaller quantities.

In a century of so much change, it is illuminating to reflect that as recently as the 1930s farm work was done mainly by hand with horse machinery. The odd crop field would be ploughed with two horses, the power and size of the huge carthorses a challenge to anyone not raised on a farm. A horse could be reasonably worked for up to six hours, throughout a long morning, ploughing up to half-an-acre a day.

There were no tractors in this area until the last war when the change to mixed farming moved apace, farmers being urged by government to plough up grassland and grow grain. Imports would become scarce during the war years. A generous government grant of £10 per acre enticed

figure 19: Reaping the harvest at Foxhill c. 1915

figure 20: Two tractors towing a threshing machine. c. 1941

*figure 21:
Mr Joe Litchfield, pictured
pre-WW1, farmed at Grange Farm*

support for this policy. Fields of wheat, oats and barley became familiar sights.

In an age before weedkillers, rows of potatoes grown for farm consumption would be hand weeded and hoed, the challenge of being first in the group to reach the end of an hour-long row, very hot and weary, maybe rewarded with a shilling.

But during the first half of the century, a hayfield would be mown with two horses, a horse drag and hay sweep. The hay would be turned, probably by hand and allowed to dry in the field. Then it was horse raked or dragged into rows, and loaded straight onto the wagon with pitchforks, before being carted off to the hayrick. If the haystack was to be built in the hayfield, the rows of hay could be swept to the stack by a horse sweep. When the stack had settled, it would be thatched with straw or reeds. Generations since the last war are not likely to have learnt the art of rick building or thatching.

At harvest time it was routine for villagers to finish their other work for the day and, with young helpers, work at the farms. Many a filled basket and large can of tea for ten has been hauled across fields by an inexhaustible farmer's wife to give the weary workers a welcome break.

As the acreages of corn-growing increased, the 'War Agricultural Committee' – set up by the Government – imported binders from America and Australia. These binders, with a man and a tractor, were hired by farmers to cut the corn. The machine would cut and tie the sheaves, and toss them on to the ground ready to be set up in stooks to dry. The corn sheaves would then be carted away and built into a corn rick or stack. The stack would be thatched or left until it was threshed, which might be at any time through to the next spring. The threshing in West Haddon was usually carried out by the Welford owner of a threshing drum.

Sheaves of corn from the stack would be pitched on to the machine and fed into it. The corn would be collected in large hessian sacks and stored, until sold or fed to animals. The full sacks of corn weighed $2^{1/4}$ hundredweight (cwt) for wheat, 2cwt for barley and $1^{1/2}$cwt for oats, and were manually handled.

West Haddon became the wartime workplace for prisoners of war, four Italians being dropped off each day to work at Grange Farm, and after their departure to work elsewhere, replaced by two landgirls who stayed at Yelvertoft, and subsequently a German prisoner. Some prisoners lived in on the farms – two at Glebe Farm, one at Grove Farm, one at Foxhill. Others lived in the hostels provided in many villages and were hired as required. The prisoners at Grove Farm and Foxhill stayed on in West Haddon after the war. They died here and are buried in the churchyard.

Changes in climate are well acknowledged. Winter as we have come to know it was then much harsher. Sheep were routinely rescued from snow drifts and in all weathers dairy cattle needed twelve-hourly milking. Lambing pens would be set up where the winter hay had already been cleared from the barn and lambing took place in March so that the ewes and lambs could go straight out into the fields. The trend towards Christmas lambing reflected the market desire for earlier lamb in the shops and the higher returns for the farmer.

Winter and summer the walls and floors of the milking shed would daily need washing down, and all equipment stripped down and sterilised, hot water carted by bucket from a tap outside the house to swill out the milking shed and the cobbled area outside.

Cows were handmilked. In winter, without the benefit of electricity, working hours would be extended by a candle propped in the side of the cowshed, or a hurricane (paraffin) lamp, both falling victim to rogue gusts of wind.

Local History Group member Ken Bailey and his wife Jean farm at Bungalow Farm. They discovered their handmilking operation was the last in the County *(fig. 22)*, and a few years ago it became the subject of a video made by the Group (supported by the British Video History Trust), which is now given twice-yearly showings on BBC2's Open University programming.

The first milking machine in the village, run by petrol engine, was installed at Glebe Farm for Jean Bailey's father, William Russell, in 'August week' (the old early-August bank holiday week), 1939.

figure 22:
Jean Bailey milking at Bungalow Farm. 1999

Being on a main route, electricity was brought to West Haddon village pre-war, but it was into the early 1950s before outlying farms received financial assistance to lay electricity supplies, with a five-year payment plan. Farmers were then encouraged to buy electric milking machines. Instances of electric lights fading when another light was switched on, ensured that candles were carried upstairs to bed even after electricity arrived to help the milking operation.

Grange Farm comprised 120 acres for many years in the early part of the century. Gradually as local farms and fields in individual ownership became available, the acreage increased to viable modern standards and it is now one of the bigger farms in this locality.

Government tax policies and subsidies over recent years have discouraged both small farmers and tenant farmers and now only one or two percent of local farms are less than 150 acres, a figure reflected nationally. As an example of the changing pattern of land ownership, farm owners within village boundaries, selling land for development at values which could never have been realised in farming, are encouraged to roll the money over into acquiring further farm land as it becomes available and avoid capital gains tax. The prices being achieved for farm land are beyond the reach of small and tenant farmers and further extend the divide between large and small farms.

The 20th Century finishes with very different problems facing those engaged in farming at the beginning of the century.

7

A West Haddon Family: the Heygates

Mary & Joe Whitty from an
interview with Miss Barbara Heygate

In 1979, during renovation work in the North Aisle, a hidden vault was discovered in the village's Norman parish church, containing the lead coffins of fifteen people. Previously unknown even to the dedicated church wardens who cared for the fabric of the building, it contained the remains of members of the Heygate family – Mary, Elizabeth, Martha, Charles, Thomas, Ann, William and others, who had died in the early 19th Century. Church warden Horace Stanley was quoted in the Northampton Chronicle at the time of the discovery saying:

'It is beautifully built... constructed using handmade red bricks of very high quality probably made in Long Buckby.' The vault was re-sealed after the renovation work was completed, but it indicates the longevity of one of West Haddon's most notable families.

There are still Heygates in West Haddon. This is something of the life, in her own words, of Miss Barbara Heygate.

"I was born at Creaton Lodge in 1924, and lived there until 1958 when my father, mother and I moved to Hardays House in West Haddon. My brother, who had already married, moved into Creaton Lodge from the cottage on the farm. My sister had already got married and moved to Surrey where she still lives.

My brother John farmed, with our father, at Creaton Lodge, Creaton, and also Sedge Hollow Farm, West Haddon and other farms in the district.

During the War I worked on the farm in the Land Army, doing any jobs that were needed, including looking after the pigs, cattle and sheep, driving the tractor, ploughing, drilling and cultivating.

Before the War, the farm was mostly grass but it was ploughed up as part of the 'Dig for Victory' campaign with the Government encouraging the country to become self sufficient in food. A lot more machinery was bought, but it was still much harder work than it is today, but very satisfying.

For many years I did the shepherding at West Haddon with the help of my dog – we would be out at first light to feed and count the stock, and also gather mushrooms, in season, for breakfast.

My father suffered a stroke in 1962, but regained much of his strength and continued to enjoy working on the farm, with which he was involved for another ten years. I nursed him when he became very ill in 1975, assisted by district nurses, at home until he died.

My mother lost a leg due to thrombosis, but after she came home from hospital she learned to walk again until a stroke confined her to a wheelchair – though she still managed to sew and cook and was a great moral support to the family until her death in 1980.

My mother and I had the bungalow, at number 1, Harday's Lane, built in 1977, with the help and advice of my brother John. My brother died very suddenly the following year – how my mother came to terms with his loss I will never know.

My nephew Roger, John's son, is married to Ann and still farms – sheep and arable – at Creaton and West Haddon. They have two sons and a daughter.

I am very proud of being one of the Heygates, a respected family in this area for many years, and I have the family tree dating back to 1558.

When the Heygate Vault was opened, I did go down to see it, and the fifteen lead coffins of family members and those they had married. The vault would have been closed since 1809.

We were made very welcome when we moved to West Haddon – my

father having been born in the village in 1889. My father was asked to become a church warden here, but he declined, having held this office at Creaton for twenty one years. We were very regular churchgoers, and I find it a great privilege and comfort to do some things to help the church now that I have the time."

figure 23:
Heygate memorial in All Saints Church

8

Charity begins at home

Mary & Joe Whitty

Looking into the history of the many and varied charitable trusts in West Haddon led us on a fascinating journey into the past, via Northamptonshire Record Office. It was a journey that which revealed the names of benefactors still familiar to residents of the village today, people who had lessened the hardships of life in the past for many villagers who were the 'industrious, deserving poor' – those with large families or who were in difficulty in their later years. The church, schoolchildren of the parish and indentured apprentices in a variety of trades were among those who also benefited. This chapter looks at some of these ancient bequests, endowments and trusts, many of which are still active today.

The documentation gives clues to the social and class structures of the past, as benefactors and trustees were given appropriate titles which indicates their places in the village hierarchy, such as twelve trustees of 1783 variously described as 'Gentleman, Drapers Yeoman, Apothecary Junior Yeoman and Surgeon', and the vicar with the rather exalted title of 'Reverend Sir and Gentleman'. Other villagers were described by way of their trades – blacksmith, woolcomber weaver, farmer, wheelwright, grazier and flax dresser.

An extract from the Charity Reports of January 1825 gives a great deal of information – including the fact that the first recorded indenture dated back to 1690.

'Whereas the two Messuages and the two quarters of a yard of land situate, lying and being in the Parish of West Haddon, in the County of Northampton, and a certain close or inclosed ground lying in Syleworth in the Parish of Watford in the County aforesaid, appointed for the relief of the poor inhabitants of the said Parish of West Haddon, and to and for such other uses for the public good and benefit of the inhabitants and parishioners of West Haddon aforesaid, have, by virtue of several indentures, been settled in Trustees for the uses aforesaid.'

This was known as the Charity Estate, and appears to have been the subject of some dispute which was settled in the High Court in the early 18th Century. The High Court was asked 'to inquire into the uses of said trusts and to redresse the misimployment of the said rents.' Unfortunately the records are silent as to the cause of the dispute!

The agreement between the minister, church wardens and thirteen villagers decreed that the rents and profits 'shall, from time to time forever hereafter be disposed of to, and for the use, benefit and advantage of the poor inhabitants of West Haddon, and for no other use, intent or purpose whatsoever.'

These are some of the charities and trusts created for the benefit of West Haddon people over the years:

~ **The Charity Estate** – founded 1690: benefactors unknown. Trustees were required to be 'able, discreet persons' and the money was for 'good and charitable and public uses'.

~ **The Apprentice Fund** – founded 1703: funded from the interest on a sum of £52 left by Jacob Lucas, Edward Barnham and another.

~ **Church Lands Charity** – an allotment of six acres, let by the church wardens to the highest bidder every six years, the rental income derived to be used for repairs to the church. The land was sold in 1988 to the Parish Council for the playing field, at a cost of £25,000; in 1997, the charity was worth some £55,000.

~ **The Kilsby Charity** – founded 1808: interest to the church Sunday School.

- **The Walker Charity** – founded 1825: £200 per annum to be applied as follows: 'One guinea to the church Sunday School, one guinea to the original Friendly Society, and the remainder to be distributed in bread and coals to the poor…'
- **John Heygate Charity** – founded 1825: built the Parochial School and a house and garden for the master and mistress; also £1000 invested for the education of the poor children of West Haddon and Winwick.
- **Heygate School Trust** (the Candlemas Charity) – founded 1837: 'John Heygate Esq. bequeathed to the School Trustees the sum of £500, the interest of which is distributed yearly at Candlemas [February 2nd] amongst the most necessitous of the poor.' Many will remember Ned Stanley, who, as church warden, would, along with the vicar, hand out the Candlemas Charity at the old Institute (the site of the present Village Hall). Only the poorest could apply. At one time, all old age pensioners in the village received £10 at Christmas. This ceased after the Charity Commissioners amalgamated several village charities.
- **Lovett Charity** – founded 1837: in 1846, this charity built the almshouses *(fig. 24)* for six aged couples. Six acres of land adjoining provided a rental income to fund repair, with the residue, if any, to be divided at Christmas among the poor of the parish aged 68 or older, or any family with five or more children under the age of ten. Because the

figure 24:
The Almshouses

57

almshouses were intended for double occupancy, sometimes two unrelated elderly people lived in them, sharing a downstairs room, which often led to conflict. The almshouses still exist on Crick Road, at the edge of the village, having been recently refurbished with replacement windows and modern conveniences.

~ **Other charitable trusts** included the John Gulliver bequest (?1861), the C.J. Slye Benefaction (1877) and the Elizabeth Heygate bequest (1888), all for the poor; the W.W. Slye Benefaction of 1903 left an endowment for a clothing club, which latterly became a savings club, both of which were administered by the church for the benefit of both church and chapel congregations.

With the advent of the welfare state, the need for charities to rescue people from extreme poverty and destitution gradually reduced. Since the war, some of the local charities have become dormant, while others have changed their objectives in a bid to provide help where it is now needed, within the spirit of the founding benefactions. In December 1972, for example, it was agreed that, given many people were using other fuels than coal to heat their homes, vouchers would be given to recipients to use as they pleased for fuel, while more recently, with the decline of traditional industry and apprenticeships, the money previously paid to apprentices would now be available to support the advancement of individual young people in the Parish.

In 1996, the decision was taken not to give a Christmas bonus, but to make money available on application to the needy – this stemmed from a review by the Charity Commissioners which questioned what purpose the grants served. The trustees reviewed the criteria and agreed that the emphasis should be more on need and should not specifically mention bread, meat or coal. The clerk to the trustees issued a notice in the Parish magazine, and spoke at length to the Darby and Joan Club. Many of the elderly claim they miss the Christmas bonus.

Most recently, grants of £100 each have been given to four young people for books to assist their studies and the Parish magazine is used to publicise the availability of grants, under the new criteria.

9

Willingly to school

Karen Biart

In researching this chapter, the bulk of the information about West Haddon Primary School came from the Headmasters' logbooks. Each had his own idea of what was important to record; some years were more informative as social history, others as stock and attendance levels. In the early years it was interesting to see how many days and half days they had off for the hunt, the flower festival or confirmations – things that nowadays happen at weekends, and a holiday each time a child of the King or Queen married, which with Queen Victoria was quite often! Without the media we have today, the children would have known little of the people they were celebrating.

With the advance of the Industrial Revolution, and increasing numbers of people eligible to vote, the need for a more educated and skilled population grew, resulting in a greater need for schools countrywide. Kelly's Directory of 1864 refers to the school in West Haddon as forming part of the National Schools Network.

Three Sunday schools, one at each of the village's places of worship, including the long gone Wesleyan chapel, also played an important part in the education of West Haddon children.

West Haddon Public Elementary School was built in 1825 and endowed by John Heygate Esq. with a house and garden for the Master and

Mistress, two adjoining cottages and the sum of £1,000, vested in Trustees. The rent from the cottages went to school funds.

The original Trust Deed for the school is dated September 2nd 1825, and there were twenty one trustees including John Heygate and six members of his family.

It was a charity school for educating and instructing the poor children of West Haddon and Winwick, between the ages of three and fourteen. The boys were to learn reading, writing, casting accounts and English grammar. The girls were also to learn knitting and plain needlework. Mr Heygate hoped that the school would run in accordance with Anglican ideals, but this view soon came under attack. In 1863 the County Court in Daventry was asked to settle the matter. The conclusion was that 'In future the school should be conducted on the principles of the Established Church but that parents were able to exempt their children from being instructed in the doctrines of the Church of England providing that they declare their conscientious objections in writing and attend another place of worship (at least once) on Sundays.'

The minutes of a Managers' meeting on October 16th 1903 stated 'Mr Griffiths is to be afforded the use of a classroom each Tuesday and Thursday morning between 9 and 9.30am, to teach whatever religious truths he desires to the children of non-conformists.'

Fees were an issue in the early life of the school. The endowment had been meant to provide for free education, and the Board of Guardians of the Parish contributed to the school's running costs. But very soon, scholars were asked to pay a contribution towards the costs of books, slates, ink and other supplies. Eventually, a scale of charges, based on social status and presumed income, was introduced, ranging from sixpence a month for the children of farmers, to thre'pence for journeymen tradesmen. Even when the adoption of the Elementary Education Act abolished fees altogether in 1891, the Chairman of the Trustees felt it necessary to urge regular attendance and highlight the benefits of the school savings bank.

Since 1952, the school has had 'controlled' status, meaning that while the County Council maintains the premises, the teaching is the responsibility of the church. The church remains very important in the life of the school, with the vicar being *ex officio*, Chairman of the Governors.

Space has always been at a premium in the school. The school inspector commented in 1892 that it was overcrowded and in need of a new classroom and a cloakroom. The school roll had grown rapidly from the time of its opening and in 1880, there were over 170 pupils. The original arrangement, with boys and girls taught in separate classes, was abandoned. Although they were now taught together, the boys and girls were still separated at playtime, as was usual for Victorian times. There was further pressure on space from the opening of the infant school in 1875.

The toilets seem to have been troublesome too, the Inspector also stated that the 'offices' (toilets) should be partitioned and the door between the two playgrounds be kept locked. The toilets were in a block on the edge of the lower school playground. Although they were improved and enlarged in 1905, they were of the 'pit' variety until 1952 when they were changed to water closets. This produced other problems, in 1956 the Head reported a problem with the WCs freezing-up and in 1968, they were covered over, making them slightly more 'comfortable' to use.

To improve lighting in the classrooms the height of the windows was raised in 1894, they were also made to open at the top. The school was heated by open fires from October to May, until replaced by stoves in 1905. This necessitated more ventilators being put into the roof. The school's only water supply came from a pump outside a house on The Green; it hardly needed pumping and often flooded.

In April 1971 the schoolhouse *(fig. 25)*, built by Mr WW Slye in 1888, was demolished to make way for new classrooms. Three new classrooms, toilets and cloakrooms were built along with two administration offices, areas for crafts, music and a library, at a cost of £25,000. Due to the difference in levels it was not possible to link the new building to the old, leaving an area of orchard between, and the school remaining as two sites.

In 1976 it seemed likely that the school would have its own kitchens and

figure 25: School with the old schoolhouse to the left

a new hall built, so that they need not rely on the village hall, but the recession halted that. The new hall finally came into being in 1998, finally linking the two parts of the school, with the old hall converted into an extra classroom and library area.

With an enlarging village bringing increasing numbers of children to the school it seems likely that services laid for phase two in 1972 will be made use of for another classroom in the near future.

Until 1955, the school year ran from November to October, with two weeks holiday at Christmas, one and a half weeks each at Easter and Whitsun, and four weeks for harvest, which varied from year to year in August or September. In addition there were days off to attend Church on Ash Wednesday, Ascension Day and for Sunday School Outings (both Chapel & All Saints), also when the school rooms were required for elections or church bazaars, before the advent of the village hall. School started with register at 8.55am (as it does a Century later), lunch from midday until 1.45pm then closing at 4pm. The hours are the same today, but lunchtime has gradually reduced to shorten the day and save on heating. Early in the Century the hours altered twice a year so that children could get home before dark (daylight saving did not come into being until 1916) and during July, to allow children to take teas up to the hayfields. On the day of the Pytchley Hunt Meet, school would close at 11.00am and reopen after lunch, this appears to have ceased by the Second World War.

Throughout the Nineteenth and first half of the Twentieth Centuries, it was common in rural areas that an important part of a family's income came from what they or their children earned working as casual agricultural labourers. Time off was given for such reasons as blackberry, pea or potato picking, or bird-scaring in fields or orchards. Amongst the girls there were also many instances of absenteeism due to having to stay home 'nursing' siblings whilst Mother worked in the fields. An 'Act to Regulate the Employment of Children in Agriculture' set out to limit the number of days a child could be absent from school for the purpose of agricultural labour. Certificates of attainment or of minimum attendance were required before a child could legally be employed during school time. An amusing log report states 'JG re-admitted on 4th to make up his attendances, left on 11th having attained required attendances under Agricultural Children's Act.'

All children had to learn the 'three Rs': reading, writing and arithmetic. Older pupils were taught singing, history and geography. Girls learnt sewing, knitting and weaving, and the boys learnt map drawing, woodwork and gardening. Whatever they produced was often sold for school funds. In 1906, pillowcases were sold for eightpence, and a kindergarten toy for a penny. Pinafores, 10d, petticoats, aprons, overalls, handkerchiefs were also made for sale.

Gardening was an important part of the curriculum *(fig. 26)*, so much so that in 1914 it was part of the Headmaster's job description. It became especially important during times of war when food was scarce. The boys grew broccoli, cauliflower, peas, cabbage and flowers for sale, and eggs were sent to both Northampton and Rugby Hospitals. A gale destroyed the

figure 26: School gardening class c. 1920s

figure 27: Woodwork class c. 1939

old toolshed in 1938, so the boys made a new one in woodwork classes *(fig. 27)*. The school was regularly visited by horticultural inspectors and received many awards for its efforts in the garden. Though the garden is long gone (it is now part of the playground), an entry in the school records for 1982 states; 'picked all the cooking apples from the tree to sell at 5p per pound for funds'.

The first school dinners were served in October 1947: 'a certain amount of equipment and provisions for a midday meal for children who have to stay has now arrived,' including cupboards, tables, towels and roller, dusters and scouring cloths. When school resumed in January 1948, nineteen children received 'Oslo' meals, so called because they originated in Norway, prepared and served by Mrs Hilda Stanley. They contained no meat, but consisted of soup, jacket 'spuds' with butter and grated cheese. Various drinks were served: Ovaltine, Bournvita and homemade fruit drinks. Puddings were apple and jam tarts, steamed pudding and milk pudding. By December 'Oslo' meals were replaced by full cooked meals, which included meat! Mrs Gardener and Mrs Osborne now joined Mrs Stanley in the canteen. All meals were cooked on paraffin stoves in one of the classrooms. By 1954, seventy children (out of 153 on the roll) were regularly eating school meals cooked and served in the Village Institute, due to lack of space on the school site. When the Institute was demolished the infants ate in the Baptist schoolroom and the older children in their classrooms until the new hall was ready. Yelvertoft kitchens then supplied the meals.

In 1970 a heavy snowfall would have meant no food but for the kindness of local farmer Ken Bailey, who managed to get through with his farm vehicle.

With catering arrangements becoming overstretched in 1976, there was a proposal to extend the school and provide a new kitchen, hall and classroom. However education cuts in the recession meant his did not happen, and by 1990 the LEA had decided to abolish school meals in favour of packed lunches.

Both wars had dramatic effects on the school. During the First, Mr

Brunner, the Headmaster, went to join the Northamptonshire Yeomanry, his position being taken by Mr Dunbar. Unfortunately for the School Managers, Mr Dunbar was then called up and had to cease acting as Head. The juniors' teacher, Mrs Kennell, was allowed leave in July 1916 to be with her husband who was home on final leave before beginning an overseas posting.

On June 18th 1919, games were organised in the playground as a peace celebration, and when school broke up for the Harvest holiday that year they were granted an extra weeks holiday by order of the King.

During the Second World War, West Haddon received evacuees – children from towns considered at risk of bombing. The already quite full school was told to expect up to a hundred extra children. The first to arrive were twenty from Barnsbury School in North London. Later, children from Ipswich would also come to the village.

Air raid drills were a fact of life even in rural Northamptonshire, Sid Adams recalls the awful sound of enemy planes passing overhead on their way to bomb Coventry. The Headmaster, Mr Latimore, was an Air Raid Warden, and supervised the childrens' drill. One time, an art lesson was abandoned so that the children could help putting tape across the windows to minimise danger from flying glass in the event of an explosion. A first aid case was also delivered, and a pump and buckets in case of incendiary bombs. From 1941, a room was made available for organising fire watches.

In 1942, there was a danger that the school railings would be requisitioned for armaments. The School Managers were extremely concerned about this, and protested that the children would be in danger from cars and that unauthorised persons could misuse the toilets in the schoolyard. The railings remained in place.

The war ended in 1945 and a sign that things were getting back to normal is the entry in August of that year reading: 'Reopened after midsummer holidays. Ninety two on roll (all natives).'!

School Day Memories

Thomas W Gare (attended 1915)

'I started at the school at three and a half and left at eleven, having won a place at Daventry Grammar School. My infant teacher was Miss Lane. The Headmaster was Mr Ash who had served in the First World War and greatly valued a small memorial with photographs of former pupils who had lost their lives in the War. His wife also taught at the school, they were strict but good teachers. I remember the War Memorial being erected and viewed with awe.'

Sue Martins – nee Wilson (attended 1948 to '58)

'I was always cold at school. If the wind was in the wrong direction the stoves weren't very warm, so we would sit with our hands up our sleeves. At break time there would be a rush to get your bottom onto the wall plate, which was at the back of the boiler, to warm up a bit.

I remember that after the registers had been taken they would be sent to the Headmasters class and the numbers recorded on a board by the bell rope.

Each Empire Day the Union Jack would be hoisted up the flag pole on the corner of the school and we would sing the National Anthem.'

Anita Rowley – nee Franzoni (attended 1970s)

'There was a tradition that on your birthday Mr Lattimore, the Headmaster gave you a thre'penny piece.

I didn't enjoy school dinners much. I remember mince with soggy cabbage and spotted dick and custard, we were always made to eat it all up.

I loved making the film 'A Walk Through West Haddon'. Mr McNulty assigned all those who wished to participate jobs. Some were actors some technicians, I was the continuity person – not a very good one! We all really enjoyed working on it.'

School Decades
with extracts from school records courtesy of
West Haddon Endowed Primary School
1870s

1874: Headmaster Mr C R Woodward assisted by Ms. L Woodward the Mistress had seventy pupils on the roll. The Inspectors report for that year was not good! 'Arithmetic a failure', and did not improve much until the arrival of a new Headmaster in 1879.

June 12th: William Elliot broke a slate carelessly this week and was sent home the next day for not paying for it.

October: Sarah Lines again forbidden to bring crochet into school. Caution: plain sewing, mending, darning or knitting, only to be brought into school!

There was much concern recorded of untidiness of the boys during this decade. Mr Woodward disciplined the pupils by excluding them, as attendance was important to gain agricultural permits and so earn much needed money for the often large families.

1880s

Colonel Percival presented the school with wall maps of the British Isles, North America, India, Australasia and the World in hemispheres.

Oct 8th 1884: HM Inspector of factories visited the school this afternoon to enquire if any breaches of the Factory Act had been committed in connection with school from the introduction of 'corset making' in the village.

In June 1899, after twenty years, Mr Crowe left the school. His style of discipline brought much criticism, from parents and Trustees, he thought unjustified. As well as caning, standing and holding a writing slate over the head was a common punishment. However the inspectors' reports improved greatly during his time, and he reintroduced singing and encouraged use of the library.

1890s

Jan 17th 1890: The Pytchley Hunt ran a fox into the village and it proved exciting to the scholars, so many stayed away that school was closed.

June 21st 1997: School was dismissed for 2½ days holiday for the Queen's Diamond Jubilee celebrations.

Bad weather and the presence of an American Exhibition and a circus kept many children from school in 1898.

1900s

The new Century got off to a 'poorly' start with many children having been absent for five weeks mainly due to scarlet fever but also whooping cough. By February whooping cough cases had increased and throughout March over half of the fifty infants were affected.

Following the death of Queen Victoria in 1901 an evening of entertainment was held in the school to raise funds for a Union Jack. In March the Hon. Mrs Fitzroy of Foxhill hoisted the Union Jack for the first time. It was hoisted again in June to commemorate the 86th anniversary of the battle of Waterloo.

1910s

Again, this decade was full of illness and epidemic causing closures through whooping cough and scarlet fever, but they still competed in the annual mid-Northants Music Competition each April.

September 23rd 1913: King George V and Queen Mary visited the area and stayed at Althorp Park as part of their Grand Tour. The children were allowed out of school to see them pass through the village.

1920s

Mr Otho Leonard Ash was Headmaster throughout the 1920s, teaching the top class of juniors. His wife Elsie taught the other Junior class.

On February 25th 1920 HRH The Prince of Wales attended the Pytchley Hunt. The staff marched the children up to The Hall to see him. A new bylaw concerning child employment came into being in that year.

In July 1924, fifty children with parents and staff visited the British Empire Exhibition at Wembley. The 4/- cost being paid by an anonymous donor.

In September 1925 the school began listening to wireless lectures *(fig. 28)*. The BBC awarded certificates to scholars who gained good marks in

figure 28: Radio lessons c. 1926

examinations, which covered many topics. In March 1927 Frank Mumford received a certificate for distinction in the wireless examination taken the previous December on geographical discoveries. Empire Day 1927 included listening to the wireless celebrations. In September Mabel Gurney and John Furniss were commended by microphone for gaining seventy two marks in the previous term's music exam by wireless.

During the summer of 1928, electric light points were installed.

1930s

Mr Edward William Lattimore from Barby took over as Headmaster in January 1936.

When King George V died on January 21st 1936, the flag was flown at half-mast. The following day it was flown high for the proclamation of King Edward VIII and the National Anthem sung. The new King did not last long – he abdicated to marry a divorcee and was succeeded by his brother, so the pupils benefited on May 11th 1937, school closed early for the Coronation of King George VI.

1940s

May 24th 1940: the ordinary timetable was suspended as usual for Empire Day observance. During the morning the lessons concentrated on Empire topics. In the afternoon parents were invited to join he staff and children in hymns and prayers, with an address from the Headmaster followed by the saluting of the flag and singing the National Anthem. There was a tableau representing Britannia and the colonies, the children then sang national songs and gave a display of dancing and skipping, and two pounds, seventeen shillings and sixpence was raised.

1950s

In 1950 there were 134 children on the roll, aged five to fourteen in 5 classes including many children aged thirteen and over from Kilsby and Crick. One of the classrooms was in the Village Institute and another in the Baptist Schoolroom.

February 6th 1952 His Majesty King George VI died. The flag was flown at half-mast and remained so until the funeral on February 15th (when two minutes silence was also observed), apart from on the day of Queen Elizabeth II's Proclamation. For both of these events, lessons were suspended in order that the children could listen to the radio broadcasts.

From 1958, children transferred at 11 years to the new secondary school at Guilsborough.

1960s

Following the purchase of a tape recorder in 1964 from school funds, the trustees purchased a television set for the children to watch schools' broadcasts in 1968.

In 1965 the LEA allowed the Headmaster to have a secretary for seven hours a week.

1970s

In April 1970 Mr Richard Young McNulty took up he post of Headmaster, taking over from Mr Lattimore, who had retired after 34 years. Mr McNulty started a parent/teacher association in September, which has proved a valuable source of extra funding over the years.

After two years of lobbying for a crossing patrol Mr Alfred Campion took up the duty of supervising the crossing of children at the beginning of 1972. Traffic passing the school was a far cry from 1909, when the headmaster had first warned of the dangers of motor vehicles.

Due to the oil crisis in 1978, a letter was received from the Secretary of State for Education with instructions to close the school when down to the last seventy gallons of oil. We were fortunate during the crisis not to lose too many days awaiting oil.

1980s

Heavy snow in January 1987 led to Miss Buttle, the acting head, sleeping at the school for two consecutive nights, in order to be sure of being there to teach.

1990s

The nineties saw the school have its first femalw Head teachers in Mrs Diane Roberts from 1994, being replaced by Mrs Jane Windsor in 1998.

The fundraising efforts of parents and the 'Friends of the School' Association have grown in importance with the decade, the money they raise providing 'extras' that augment the basic schooling. A new avenue was found to provide a badly needed football strip – sponsorship from big business.

A sad sign of he times is that security systems had to be installed following an increase in thefts and incidents where intruders attacked staff and pupils at other schools.

The school was first visited by a team of Ofsted inspectors in 1995, the report being in the main good. The school continues to grow, largely due to new housing developments along the Guilsborough Road, and looks likely to remain, alongside the Parish Church and the Village Hall, as a focal point for village life.

10 A changing century

Annie Ballantyne

It is the final hour of the final century of the second millennium.

In homes around the village, year-end traditions are being upheld. But this is an occasion unlike others, made special by a community joining together in celebration.

Front doors are opening onto streets wet from earlier rain. Warmly clad figures emerge and make their way down Guilsborough Road and up Station Road, along High Street and West End, to mingle on The Green. As any local will tell you, The Green has long foregone its origins in favour of the 20th Century need for vehicle parking space. The village school is in comfortable darkness. Alongside, in the village hall, a huge party is in happy mood. Initiated by two community minded people, who did not want anyone to be alone if it was not their choice, the numbers swelled to sixty. Candlelit dinner has been cleared and now they dance to favourite melodies of the past century. Some are enticed to join the procession now wending its way towards All Saints' Church.

The church is floodlit, providing easy passage up the long flight of wide steps. We climb past the memorial honouring the dead of two World Wars, and the shadowy tombstones from centuries past, remembering those who have given hope and future to our community. The church is filling, a smiling and thoughtful line of villagers moves up the central aisle to light

73

individual candles from the tall Millennium Candle. On the stroke of midnight the bells commence their peel, practiced throughout the seasons by an enthusiastic group determined that this church, like many others throughout the land, would ring out a message of hope. A cheer is raised from those waiting outside. A few moments of prayer and then the bells ring out again and the flickering lights of candles, lanterns and torches lead us up High Street and on to the playing field. Many ages between young and old, from those in pushchairs to those with walking sticks.

Earlier in the day a huge bonfire has been skillfully built by volunteers and it blazes now, cascading sparks into the night sky. Old friends and new greet each other and from near and far fireworks trace fiery trails and explode overhead.

The day dawns bright. The village is quiet. On a footpath across fields farmed through the centuries, a party of walkers hears the bells of neighbouring villages join ours in celebrating a new century. A new millennium. A new page in history.

figure 23:
Village children look towards the future

Several versions of the following rhyme exist about the village:

> *Cobbler Dunkley on the hill,*
> *Mr Gilbert sits quite still,*   (...Miss Hill's)
> *Tumky Vernon keeps the pub,*   (...in Station Road)
> *Precious Jewell just above,*
> *Mr Palmer keeps three geese,*
> *Bobby Fitzhugh is our police,*
> *Potter Furniss on the square,*   (...tailor)
> *Tommy Adams keeps china*
>   *& earthenware,*
> *Puffer Adams the grand Co-op,*
> *Mr Farn the saddler's shop,*
> *Just above the grand hotel,*   (...The Crown)
> *Where King Woodford*
>   *loved to dwell.*

Other versions include Dr Harday and Miss Seal. Perhaps it was a children's skipping song? It has been handed down through the years and some of the characters you'll now recognise. And the others? Well that's another story and another book...

West Haddon Local History Group
Summer 2000

76